WONDERMENTS
OF THE EAST BAY

Sylvia Linsteadt and Malcolm Margolin

With contributions by
Lindsie Bear, Grace Carroll, Michael Drake,
Marilee Enge, Vincent Medina, and Gayle Wattawa

Heyday, Berkeley, California

To the Wild Ones of our valleys, hills, and woods.—SL

To Jerry Kent, retired assistant general manager of the East Bay Regional Park District, whose friendship has sustained me and whose devotion to the District continues to inspire me.—MM

© 2014 by Heyday

Parts of "Rock Walls" are reprinted from *The East Bay Out* (updated edition) by Malcolm Margolin (Berkeley: Heyday, 1988).

Map on the inside front cover is courtesy of the East Bay Regional Park District.

Library of Congress Cataloging-in-Publication Data
Linsteadt, Sylvia, author.
  Wonderments of the East Bay / Sylvia Linsteadt and Malcolm Margolin ; with contributions by Lindsie Bear [and 5 others].
     pages cm
  ISBN 978-1-59714-296-0 (pbk. : alk. paper)
  1. Natural history--California--East Bay. 2. Natural history--California--East Bay Regional Park District. 3. East Bay Regional Park District (Calif.) I. Margolin, Malcolm, author. II. Title.
  QH76.5.C2L56 2014
  508.794--dc23

                                        2014019248

Cover Photo: Anna's hummingbird perched on sage, by Rick Lewis
Cover Design: Ashley Ingram
Interior Design/Typesetting: Ashley Ingram and Rebecca LeGates

Orders, inquiries, and correspondence should be addressed to:
            Heyday
            P.O. Box 9145, Berkeley, CA 94709
            (510) 549-3564, Fax (510) 549-1889
            www.heydaybooks.com

Printed in California

10 9 8 7 6 5 4 3 2 1

CONTENTS

ACKNOWLEDGMENTS

First and foremost, the authors would like to thank the East Bay Regional Park District—in particular Robert Doyle, Carol Johnson, Brenda Montano, and David Zuckerman—for supporting this project in honor of its eightieth anniversary and in general for protecting, preserving, and accommodating wonderment during its stewardship. Jerry Ting and Rick Lewis provided many of the stunning photographs in the book and deserve special mention. The wonderful map of the parks is courtesy of Kara Hass. Molly Woodward copyedited this book on-site at Tilden, and Lisa K. Marietta did a thorough proofread. Thanks to Michael Drake for fact-checking, Jack Laws for inspiration and advice, and the staff of Heyday for making it all such fun.

Burrowing owl at
Arrowhead Marsh

INTRODUCTION

Malcolm Margolin

It's April in Tilden Regional Park. "I've never seen a spring as beautiful as this," I say to Rina, my wife and hiking companion, as we walk through a meadow bursting with wildflowers. She nods her agreement and, unfailingly kind, refrains from reminding me that I've been saying the exact same thing every year for the fifty years we've been together. Is the world evolving toward greater beauty? It's possible, I suppose. But what is more likely is that as I grow older my capacity to appreciate and celebrate beauty has been expanding.

This book of "wonderments" is a birthday present and love letter to a longtime friend and constant companion, the East Bay Regional Park District, which turns eighty this year. The District has played a major role in my life from the day I first visited Berkeley in 1967 to the present. I worked at Redwood Regional Park for three years in the early 1970s, and my first two books grew out of that experience. In the years since, the 114,000 acres and sixty-five parks that comprise the East Bay Regional Park District have served as an art gallery, a museum, a university, a gymnasium, a concert hall, a shrine, and a playground. I feel that my limbs are still strong from constantly hiking in the hills, my ideas more capacious, my love of beauty deeper, and my family more tightly knit because of these parks.

I am writing these lines early on a Sunday morning. Soon, others will be awake, picnic baskets will be packed, children and grandchildren will be rounded up, and this curious assemblage of humans called a "family" will head off to Tilden for a day of hiking, eating together, looking at the spring wildflowers, and giving the kids a ride on the Steam Train. I have from the day I arrived here been grateful to those who conceived of this Park District and to the extraordinary vision and civic devotion of those who, in 1934, at the height of the Great Depression, voted to raise their taxes so that they and future generations would be able to enjoy this land.

While this book is a song of praise for the animals, plants, and lands of the East Bay Regional Parks, I think of it also as a homage to the amazing time in which we live. I find myself endlessly astonished by the explosion of facts, knowledge, and information that is now so easily available to us. When I started writing and publishing some forty years ago, information was still scarce and hard to come by. Door-to-door salesmen offered multivolume encyclopedias on an installment plan, and those who had such a set were the envy of all. If you wanted to know something about redwood trees, you could look in the *Encyclopedia Britannica,* Volume 9, and there on page 990 was a three-paragraph article. Today you can Google "redwood trees" and in two seconds have access to nearly two and a half million entries. What a feast for the hungry mind! We can indeed gorge ourselves on facts, and some of those facts are simply wondrous.

But while the wealth of facts has indeed enriched this book and enriched my life, the overload of unmediated information tends to clog and dull the mind, and I further view this book as a homage to the power, perhaps even the necessity, of art and of language. Wallace Stegner once made this fascinating observation: "No place, not even a wild place, is a place until it has had that human attention that at its highest reach we call poetry." The writing of this book, especially my collaboration with my coauthor, Sylvia Linsteadt, has been a joy. Sometimes I would write something, sometimes she would. Often, though, I would spin stories and unfurl ideas, she would add thoughts of her own, and by some alchemical process she'd spin it all into gold. Sensing that we were having fun, other members of Heyday's staff (Lindsie Bear, Grace Carroll, Michael Drake, Marilee Enge, Vincent Medina, and Gayle Wattawa) added chapters of their own. Diane Lee and Ashley Ingram scoured the world for photos. In her role as editor, Gayle Wattawa tamed the extravagance and strengthened the spirit of this book. Wonderments begat wonderments.

Needless to say, this slender book falls short of being complete, and it may very well fall short of even being adequate. This "dewdrop world" of ours, as the Japanese poet Issa calls it, is miraculous and fleeting, its multitude of mysteries beyond our understanding. These few pages do not seek to define what might be wondered at. What you have before you is at best a sampling, an overture, an invitation to explore and to wonder.

While we found some truly fine wonderments, we barely skimmed the surface. There are thousands more. Accept this book as an invitation to find some of your own. And as you rejoice at the great beauty and wonder of the world, know that you, your family, and your friends, too, are wonderments. Accept it, enjoy it, and please use that awareness to celebrate beauty and to create a just, abundant, loving, and merciful world.

Acorn woodpecker
pounding an acorn
into a tree

ACORN
WOODPECKERS

Acorn woodpeckers, bright capped, gregarious, and chatty, are common residents of the oak woodland of Sunol-Ohlone Regional Wilderness, where they can be seen dipping in flight from one tree to the next. Their raucous calls resemble high-pitched, lonesome laughter, and one wonders what these jester-like birds communicate to one another. The location of good grub? The intrusion of marauding scrub jays? Quite possibly family gossip! For above all things, acorn woodpeckers are social birds, organized in large families around communally tended acorn granaries, controlling up to fifteen-acre territories.

Melanerpes formicivorus seems to be constantly working. He gathers acorns in the fall and pounds them into holes he has drilled in the bark of oaks, pines, and other trees. One tree may have thousands of holes, each containing a single acorn. Large trees are something like savings banks, grand institutions where the provident woodpecker deposits the bounty of fall in anticipation of the lean months ahead. Storing so many acorns is a lot of work, not only because scrub jays love nothing better than a stolen luncheon but also because as acorns dry they shrink, and must be relocated to newer, snugger holes for proper storage.

These thrifty habits ensure food throughout the year, and acorn woodpeckers are almost always year-round residents of this place. Perhaps the need to maintain and defend this concentrated food source is related to the unusual communal nesting practices of acorn woodpeckers. Babies are raised by up to seven males and two or three females at once, and often a single nest contains chicks from different fathers and mothers. Generally, fathers in a nest group are brothers, and mothers are sisters, though these brothers and sisters are unrelated. Grown offspring will hang around their natal nest until the next mating season, acting as nursery helpers.

Not surprisingly, a complex arrangement like this is fraught with tension. Despite cooperation to raise young, competition is intense: males are known to interrupt one another's mating efforts, and females may destroy eggs not their own. In fact, more than a third of the eggs laid each season are crushed or pushed out of the nest.

On spacious hillsides dotted by oaks, the acorn woodpeckers' autumn hammering and boisterous calls thrum out an old, old song. If one listens long enough, one might separate the strands of juveniles beseeching mothers and aunts, fathers and uncles; lovers calling out to their myriad mates; sentinels signaling an onslaught of scrub jays; and grandmothers quarrelling amongst themselves. Clamorous and exuberant, it is nothing less than the music of life on earth.

Sylvia Linsteadt

Acorn woodpeckers abound in the oak woodlands of many of the East Bay Regional Parks, including Sunol Regional Wilderness.

Top: Acorn granary
Bottom: Acorn woodpecker

Formica aerata

ANTS

A terrible war is being waged in our backyards. The belligerents: the diverse native ant populations and the invading legions of Argentine ants (*Linepithema humile*).

In the early 1890s, a founding population of Argentine ants was accidently carried from South America into New Orleans by coffee freighters. Since then, these ants have gone on to become one of the most successful invasive species of the modern world. Thriving in Mediterranean climates, massive populations have sprouted up in Japan, the Mediterranean proper, and here in California, where they first arrived in 1907. The San Francisco Bay Area is at the heart of an Argentine ant supercolony dubbed "The California Large," which is measured in the hundreds of billions of ants and stretches for more than five hundred miles. While most ant species operate at the hive level and quarrel with neighboring nests, Argentine ants are so genetically homogenous that ants from far-removed hives will greet each other as sisters. When each nest contains hundreds of thousands of individuals and several reproductive queens, it becomes clear how vast networks arise.

Surprisingly, the Argentine ant has been able to wrest control of California from our incumbent ants. Argentine ants are small—their workers a paltry three millimeters—whereas among the more than one hundred species of ants native to the East Bay are some large and ferocious competitors. Carpenter ants of the genus *Camponotus* are several times the size of Argentine ants and possess a terrifying bite. John Muir wrote, "I fancy that a bear or wolf bite is not to be compared with it. A quick electric flame of pain flashes along the outraged nerves, and you discover for the first time how great is the capacity for sensation you are possessed of." Perhaps

Top: Carpenter ant
Bottom: Ants on manzanita blossoms

more insidious are our local *Polyergus* ants, which raid the nests of lesser *Formica* species, stealing eggs and larvae and coercing their new slaves to maintain their nests. On occasion, a *Formica* queen is even held hostage, controlled by a *Polyergus* queen until she lays a sufficient number of eggs, after which she is dispatched. Also included in our local palette of ants are centipede-hunting specialists, spider-egg robbers, and even fungus farmers.

This colorful diversity has been the undoing of our native ants. Different species are more enemy than ally and have coexisted by niche partitioning. Faced with the onslaught of Argentine ants, our fractured native ants, for all their individual feistiness, are simply overrun. Argentine ants storm one by one the nests of their enemies in a wave, ripping inhabitants to shreds. Entire species disappear as the Argentine ants march ever forward.

Michael Drake

While Argentine ants dominate human-disturbed environments, like suburban lawns, our Regional Parks have become a bastion for native California ants. Native ant populations can still be found in virtually all protected wilderness areas of the East Bay Regional Parks.

Top: Godwits, teal, and dowitchers over Arrowhead Marsh
Bottom, left to right: Skunk, squirrel, Monarch butterfly

ARROWHEAD MARSH

Named for its aerial resemblance to an Indian artifact, Arrowhead Marsh lies within the shadow of the Oakland Airport and its surrounding industrial landscape of warehouses and factories. Given its location, you might expect to find blight, trash, odors, and oil slicks.

Think again.

Take a midday walk around the marsh loop. You'll be joined by joggers on short sprints through their lunch breaks, mothers pushing strollers, airplane mechanics stretching cramped muscles, birders, and badass teens cutting class. Depending on the season, your companions may also include an eclectic mix of skinny-legged shorebirds—willets, avocets, stilts, and dowitchers—picking their way along the water's edge in search of small fish; greater white-fronted

Ridgway's rail

geese on a rare stopover; cinnamon teal, scaup, canvasbacks and ruddy ducks dabbling in the channel; and ground squirrels popping from manmade crevasses in the concrete riprap to snag a bit of a picnic lunch. Songbirds like marsh wrens and sparrows trill from the coyote bush. A mother and father mallard try to distract passersby from a hidden nest. Often, there's the astonishing sight of a lone great blue heron known for his mammal-hunting prowess; poised motionless over a gopher hole, his practice is one of marvelous patience. The patches of native sticky monkey-flower and blue-eyed grass are the handiwork of restoration volunteers. All in all, Arrowhead Marsh reminds us that, given a chance, the natural world can not only hang on in the midst of human activity, it can flourish.

Marilee Enge

Arrowhead Marsh can be found within Martin Luther King Jr. Regional Shoreline, a 741-acre park protecting rare wetland ecosystems.

Anna's hummingbird
perched on sage

Top: Godwits
Bottom, left to right: Barn swallow, brown pelican

Western long-eared myotis drinking

BATS

When dusk gathers, lilac-blue, the bats come out on deft and silken wings. Sometimes they are so quick you can hardly see them, just a soft flash of darkness as they dart over reservoirs, hunting insects by that language of sound and distance called echolocation. Although myths abound of the blindness of bats and of the dangers of getting them tangled in your hair, in fact most bats have decent spatial awareness. They use echolocation because it is *more* accurate than sight for catching quick and diminutive waterside insects such as mosquitoes.

It's the same principle as the echo that follows your bellow into a canyon. What we perceive as clicks are bats' high-pitched harmonic noises, which move out like waves and bounce back after

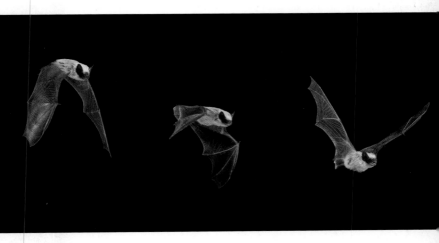

Western canyon bat

Top, left to right: Townsend's big-eared bat, pallid bat
Bottom: California leaf-nosed bat

encountering solid matter. A bat's ears—alert and often large—are designed to gather up that echo like a telegram and read it quick as a flash. These sonic encodings describe not only where an object is in space but also which species it is and more—which fruit or insect, whether flowers are full or empty of nectar. Each click brings the bat new data about nearby hazel trees and willow branches, wily mosquitoes and roosting ducks, just as our eyes would take it all in.

A bat's wing, webbed and taut like the most delicate of umbrellas, is actually an arm bone attached to an elongated hand with spindly fingers joined by skin. The claws that bats use to hang and crawl across cave ceilings are their thumbs. This combination of arm-and-hand structure with wing structure is brilliant design: with their wing-hands, bats can tack and turn and bob and weave through the air at quicksilver speeds in pursuit of the tiniest of bugs.

The Bay Area boasts over fifteen species of these miraculous flying mammals. In a recent survey at Del Valle Regional Park, the Park District's bat specialist, Jessica Sheppard, counted over one thousand bats in a single evening exiting from specially made bat boxes. Every evening, each bat eats half its bodyweight in insects as it fills the dusk with gentle hunting songs, its little voice echoing, mapping the starry night.

Sylvia Linsteadt

Bats are best seen at dusk, when they hunt for insects over Lake Chabot, Shadow Cliffs, or Lake Del Valle.

Beaver eating, Martinez

BEAVERS

The homecoming of a beaver, its wide tail steering it to a creek bed, riparian alley, or marsh, is a blessing. It's a song of relief for the willows who've been waiting for those pruning teeth. The spawning salmon and hungry herons also chime in their thanks.

Although we don't think of this area as beaver country, golden beavers (*Castor canadensis subauratus*) were once especially abundant in the Delta, where they tunneled into the sandy banks of the myriad tiny rush-covered islands until fur trappers from the Hudson Bay Company, who arrived in Northern California around 1828, slaughtered them in staggering numbers for their pelts. Later classified as undesirable rodents and never protected by closed hunting seasons, golden beavers virtually vanished from the area by the end of the twentieth century.

Then, like magic, in 2006 a pair of beavers set up residence in Alhambra Creek in downtown Martinez, a city near the Delta. Nobody was sure why. They came regardless of the creek's depletion and set about making house. Reactions were mixed: beavers are notorious tree fellers and flood makers, and in a town that had recently spent $10 million for flood-proofing, not everyone saw this ecological homecoming as cause for celebration.

City council members wanted to exterminate the young beaver couple straightaway, but something remarkable happened. Visitors began to flood Martinez, drawn wholly by the beavers. They'd peer over the side of the bridge to catch a glimpse of the beavers carrying freshly cut cottonwood and willow to their new home. School buses full of children arrived. Townspeople vehemently protested any harm to the beavers. After months of deliberation, the Martinez City Council relented and called in a beaver flood-control expert

Top: Beaver, Martinez
Bottom: Alhambra Creek footbridge

from Vermont. He installed a pipe in the dam that lowered the water level, thereby tricking the beavers into maintaining a smaller dam.

Within a month of their arrival, the beaver pair gave birth to three babies and had meanwhile become thoroughly beloved by Martinez residents, most notably Heidi Perryman, founder of the Martinez Beavers website, where regular updates about the beavers can be found. Not only do the beavers of Martinez provide endless stories—the original mother beaver died in 2010, but lo, her mate went away a few months later and came back with a new wife!—they also have transformed Alhambra Creek for the better. The creek is once again a thriving wildlife corridor, with beaver ponds supporting the return of steelhead trout, river otters, and minks, and the appearance of the first tule perch ever recorded in Alhambra Creek. Beavers, after all, are ecological architects: Their damming and pond-making creates and sustains bodies of water between creek and meadow that would otherwise be dry. Their tree-trimming encourages cottonwoods and willows to grow back bushy, thus providing safe roost for migratory birds. The still, oxygenated water of their ponds is the perfect breeding ground for rare East Bay amphibians, such as red-legged frogs, and a vital habitat for young coho salmon.

When the beavers returned, they brought bounty on their golden backs, ushering the rebirth of a languishing creek bed.

Sylvia Linsteadt

Beavers have been consistent inhabitants of the Delta, and healthy beaver populations can also be found among the tidal sloughs of Big Break Regional Shoreline.

Top and bottom: Belgum Sanitarium, founded 1914

BELGUM
SANITARIUM

On a late summer day the pears are still pendulous as they hang from unpruned trees, and the blackberries have gone feral in thickets dark with fruit. Under the shade of overgrown palms, cows rest and chew their cud. A hundred years ago, these pear trees and their companion apple trees, equally scruffy, provided sustenance for the motley crew of residents at the now-vanished Belgum Sanitarium, an insane asylum for the relations of wealthy Bay Area urbanites.

Founded in 1914 as the Grande Vista Sanitarium by Dr. Hendrik Belgum, it remained in his hands until a grass fire in 1948 threatened the house and he died trying to put it out. The estate and a few remaining patients passed into the hands of his brother, Bernard, and his spinster sisters, Ida and Christine, none of whom had any psychiatric or medical qualifications. When Bernard died in 1963, no heirs were left to inherit the estate, and it was abandoned. Fifteen years later, the East Bay Regional Park District added the land to the existing Wildcat Canyon Regional Park that surrounded it. By then, all the remaining buildings had burned to the ground, and today only a few stone foundations and a handful of exotic palms, fruit trees, and herbs remain of the strange madhouse-Eden that, for a brief fifty years, flourished here.

Everything about the Belgum Sanitarium has the ring of odd enchantment to it, the glint of something rare and tragic and beautiful. The land is gentle and sloping here at the far northern end of Wildcat Canyon Regional Park, with beautiful views out over the Bay toward San Francisco, Mount Tamalpais, and Richmond. In

Top: Belgum Sanitarium
Bottom: Palm trees at Belgum Sanitarium site today

the early 1900s, when the Bay's edges were still largely undeveloped, these vistas must have felt transcendent. Dr. Belgum seemed to have taken the whole health of his patients into consideration, not only locating his sanitarium in the sanctuary of an oak forest but also nurturing an oasis-homestead of apiaries, dairy cows, fruit orchards, a vegetable garden, and a private spring.

It is said that local children who snuck around the edges of the sanitarium at dusk often heard eerily beautiful music played on clarinets or pianos or horns coming from the windows of the main house. Apparently Dr. Belgum regularly held musical evenings with his patients, and he and his two sisters, who were often described as "ethereal," joined in the dancing. In his later years, it was also said that Dr. Belgum rarely ventured out, preferring the company of his patients—and perhaps also the peace of his oak-edged estate tucked above Wildcat Creek, where the fog rested nightly in summer and the ever-increasing bustle and noise of the Bay's cities still felt far away.

The abandoned Belgum Sanitarium is a place where it seems possible that a wayward hiker, gathering blackberries along the carriage-path entry late in the summer dusk, might hear faint music still haunting the air as the lights of the city of Richmond below flicker on, one by one.

Sylvia Linsteadt

The Belgum Sanitarium's foundations and what's left of the surrounding gardens can still be viewed off the Belgum Trail at the north end of Wildcat Canyon Regional Park.

Yellow-faced bumblebee on a manzanita blossom

BUZZ
POLLINATION

Crooners in nightclubs, guitarists on street corners, sopranos at the opera all make their living by making music—all, in effect, singing for their supper. So do certain bumble bees in search of pollen.

Pollen is formed within the part of a flower called an anther. In most flowers, the anther splits open lengthwise, releasing its pollen and making things easy for a visiting bee. Some plants, however—among them manzanitas, huckleberries, and shooting stars—withhold their pollen, keeping it tightly inside the anther with a thread of static electricity. They release it reluctantly and only through small pores at the tip of the anther.

To collect such hard-to-get pollen, certain species of bumble bees and digger bees have evolved a remarkable technique known as buzz pollination. A female worker bee approaches the flower, grabs onto it with her legs and mandibles, and with her wings at rest, shivers her huge internal flight muscles, which by some anatomical mystery are detached from her wings. This movement causes her thorax to vibrate rapidly like a tuning fork, creating a high-pitched sound audible to the human ear. The anther trembles in harmony and releases the pollen in small clouds like puffs of talcum powder. To top it off, much of the pollen is attracted to the hairy body of the bee by a negative charge generated by the bee's activity.

Sylvia Linsteadt

Buzz-pollinated plants can be found en masse at Huckleberry and Sobrante Ridge Regional Preserves.

Manzanita blossoms

Left to right: Shooting star, yellow-faced bumblebee on a solanum blossom

Flame skimmer

DRAGONFLIES

With their jewellike bodies, delicate wings, and nervous flight, it's easy to think of dragonflies as frail trinkets of the insect world. But wander along the bank of Lake Chabot or San Pablo Bay's Breuner Marsh and watch these divas closely. The dragonfly has evolved over 350 million years into a perfect killing machine.

In small ponds without the threat of big fish, dragonflies reign at the top of the food chain. Mature ones hunt ruthlessly, eating almost any flying insect smaller than themselves, including weaker brethren. Many species of dragonflies flourish in the Bay Area, including grappletails, great spreadwings, common green darners, western pondhawks, and blue dashers. On warm summer days, behold the aerial duels of male dragonflies: dipping, darting, and diving with machismo, these ceremonial "fights" over a prime

Variegated meadowhawk

Top: Common green darner
Bottom: Blue dasher

patch of water lilies or a mossy bank are more showmanship than combat. The dragonfly's set of four muscular wings, each independently moving, allows him to fly backward and upside down, rotate 360 degrees midflight, and reach speeds of up to thirty miles an hour before stopping on a dime. This dexterity spells success in almost 98 percent of attacks, making the insects more effective hunters than great white sharks and African lions.

Dragonflies begin their lives underwater, where they hatch and then endure a nymph stage for several years. Unlike other squishy aquatic larvae, dragonfly nymphs are born tough. They are strong enough to catch and consume tadpoles and even small fish, and their faces are covered with extendable mouthpieces that unfurl to spear unsuspecting prey and gather them into the predators' mouths. Scuttling along the bottom of still ponds, the nymphs move through the water by anal jet propulsion, pulling water into the anus (they breathe via rectal gills), then expelling the water at high pressure, which shoots them forward.

The dragonfly is steeped in more mythology than any other insect except perhaps the butterfly. Wherever the dragonfly thrives, humans have built up legends and folktales about its origin and purpose. Mothers once warned naughty children about the "devil's darning needle" that just might fly into an open bedroom window at night and stitch a liar's mouth shut. The dragonfly lives up to his medieval namesake: the East Bay is full of tiny, fearsome dragons.

Grace Carroll

The best time to view dragonflies is on warm summer days, when they can be found perched on reeds or hovering over ponds in parks across the East Bay.

Blue elderberries with an insect visitor

ELDERBERRIES

The sight of a blue elderberry in full bloom some late spring afternoon arrests the world's movement for an instant. Her slender, arching branches haloed by sweet white umbels sway in a small wind; the bees hum, delighted; the sun catches the white blossoms; and you can finally breathe again. For the indigenous people of this land, the blossoming and ripening of our native blue elderberry (*Sambucus nigra* ssp. *caerulea*) were important calendar markers. We often think first of plants' ethnobotanical uses—the medicine in their roots, the uses of their bark, fiber, and fruit—and the blue elderberry is certainly queen among plants in these regards. But in that older world, she was perhaps foremost a timekeeper.

When elderberry flowers bloomed, this signaled to the native people of the Bay Area the end of the shellfish season. No more could be gathered until the elderberry flowers turned to dusty black berries at the cusp of summer and fall. In between, during the dry summer months, shellfish were subject to the red tides caused by algal blooms, which made them toxic to humans. But this isn't merely a convenient way to remember dates: some years, the elderberry blossoms earlier than others. It is affected by the same seasonal factors as the red tides of offshore algal blooms, just as the comings and goings of songbirds are connected to peaks and dips in temperature and light. This way of seeing time is rooted squarely in the living phenomena of the world, in the web of connection that hitches each thing to the next.

We've stepped out of this flow of time; we've cut up time into even numbers and precise dates that have little to do with what's going on in the living world right around us. The elderberry is a doorway out of mechanical time, leading us back into the rhythms

Top: Chestnut-backed chickadee with blue elderberries
Bottom: Blue elderberry blossoms

of a natural time punctuated by mysteries like the moment of blossom, the moment the golden-crowned sparrow returns, the moment of fruit.

The elderberry was also a more literal timekeeper in the older world of native California: her light branches were made into clapper sticks that beat out a rhythm, sounding time to the dancer's feet. And so she both marks and measures the passage of time.

The world over, elderberry's hollow branches have been used for musical instruments—in fact, the name *Sambucus* comes from the ancient Greek *sambuke,* a stringed instrument likely made from elderberry wood. Here in native California, elderberry flutes were used for courting. It was said that to select the right branch for flute making and wooing, you had to find a tree with music in it. In order to do that, you waited for a windless day, and then you wandered until you found an elderberry with a leaf moving in the still air. Such a tree had music held inside. It is a reminder that music resides in the world, and we may only coax it out. When we do, that music reconnects us to elderberry-time, giving us a glimpse of the calendar of the living land.

Sylvia Linsteadt

The rugged and aptly named Elderberry Trail of Las Trampas Regional Wilderness is a wonderful place to experience spring's elderberry blooms.

Eucalyptus trees with peeling bark

EUCALYPTUS

The silver-gold eucalyptus tree, with its blue and spired leaves, casts a rustling glow. With straight, smooth trunks and ever-peeling bark, these trees stand with regal, lonely splendor. Due to the volatile oils in their roots, which they excrete into the surrounding soil, not much else grows where the eucalyptus grows, at least not in its introduced habitat here in California.

Despite its austerity and grandeur, this tree has a mixed reputation, and for good reason—it is invasive and also a fire hazard. Eucalyptus groves are common throughout the East Bay Regional Parks (mainly comprised of the Tasmanian blue gum variety, *Eucalyptus globulus*), where you'll see piles of aromatic bark like scraps of cloth and hear the papery chime of wind in the leaves. These

Cedar waxwing atop eucalyptus flowers

Top: Old eucalyptus tree
Bottom, left to right: Eucalyptus flowers, flowers with hooded oriole

native Australians are here to stay, just like those of us humans with ancestors from other lands.

In Australia, eucalyptus trees (or gum trees, as they are called there) have been held sacred by Aboriginal peoples since the beginning of time; this is the tree that holds up the big blue dome of the sky in Dreamtime myths. And like the limbs of our native elderberry, the eucalyptus also has music in her branches: the Aboriginal didgeridoo, a sacred and shamanic instrument, is made from hollowed young eucalyptus trunks, and remains central in ceremonies to this day.

The eucalyptus is a living medicine chest—you can tell just by breathing the nearby air, which is spiced with those volatile oils, so wonderful at relieving congestion, at combating viruses and other infections, and at cleaning wounds. In that hushed blue shade and sweet-sharp smell of leaf and bark, there is a simple beauty to be found, a reminder that sometimes the names we give—native, nonnative, good, bad—blind us to the inherent wonders of each plant and tree and animal and stone.

Sylvia Linsteadt

Claremont Canyon Regional Preserve, once the site of several eucalyptus plantations, is home to thousands of eucalyptus trees and is the center of the East Bay's eucalyptus-removal debate.

Ground squirrel

GROUND SQUIRRELS AND RATTLESNAKES

It's like something from a book of stories: the ground squirrel—wily, golden-furred burrower of the open meadows and prairies of the West—anoints herself with the rank perfume of her mortal enemy, the Pacific rattlesnake, to mask her own smell, often effectively fooling the serpent into passing over her tunnel, her hibernaculum, and her nest full of tiny new babies. The California ground squirrel (*Otospermophilus beecheyi*) has been in a coevolutionary dance with the Pacific rattlesnake (*Crotalus oreganus*) for some fifteen million years, since ancestral ground squirrels descended from tree branches and braved the meadows and the underground. But ground squirrel babies are a favorite dish among rattlesnakes, perfectly timed for their May–June emergence from winter torpor.

Most of the ground squirrels' defensive behavior seems to have been developed to protect their young, as adult ground squirrels don't often fall prey to poisonous snakes. Scientists at UC Davis have spent the last thirty years studying the interactions between ground squirrels and their predators. Certain populations of California ground squirrels develop an immunity to rattlesnake venom by the age of one month, which in turn causes local populations of rattlesnakes to up the ante with more potent venom. Squirrels are incredibly nimble at avoiding rattlesnake bites, and even seem to initiate aggressive interactions by kicking sand and waving tails pumped full of warm blood. This startles rattlesnakes into retreat; they mainly use infrared vision (in addition to smell) when hunting, and interpret this sudden quick banner of heat as belonging to a much larger animal.

All of this scolding and harassment inspires the rattlesnake to rattle its infamous tail, and the offending ground squirrel can discern the length and vigor of the snake by the loudness of the rattle. The squirrel then notifies his brethren, calling for reinforcements if need be. If all of this doesn't deter the snake from tunnels and nests, hopefully some snakeskin musk will. A squirrel will bathe in the dust where a rattlesnake recently slept to pick up its smell, or even chew up previously shed rattlesnake skins and then lick its paws, tunnels, and babies in the hope that a marauding snake will smell another rattler and, not wanting to cause conflict, head elsewhere for dinner.

Despite the arsenal of defenses ground squirrels have developed to combat their own dragon, their newborn offspring still make up about 70 percent of a rattlesnake's diet in spring and early summer. And so the ancient battle-dance of snake and squirrel spirals onward as each regularly ingests the other in one way or another.

Sylvia Linsteadt

Ground squirrels nest in grassland environments and are easily found in Round Valley Regional Preserve.

Top: Ground squirrels
Middle and bottom: Pacific rattlesnake

Ladybug

LADYBUGS

Why does the sight of hundreds, if not hundreds of thousands, of overwintering ladybugs fill us with spine-tingling awe? During the colder months at Redwood Regional Park, this is a familiar sight for hikers: convergent ladybugs (*Hippodamia convergens*) huddled together for warmth in shared diapause—insect hibernation—on select logs, trees, and foliage. Though they barely move when chilled, the ladybugs come alive when temperatures rise, lumbering about and mating.

Perhaps our joy is owing to the ladybug itself, that rotund and jolly harbinger of luck and aphid-free gardens. In spite of our affection for it, nothing about the ladybug, or "ladybird beetle," as entomologists would prefer you say, is designed solely for human happiness. Its cheerful coloration, which recalled the shawls of Our Lady Mary in European iconography (hence "lady" bugs), is really a warning sign to predators: eat me and prepare for a nasty-tasting meal. The ladybug bleeds toxins from its leg joints when attacked. Its pleasingly round shape? An armored tank to repel ants and other threats.

Maybe our delight stems from the scale of their presence: we're talking thousands of beetles, maybe even millions. The ladybug is solitary over the spring and summer months, as it single-mindedly gorges on aphids in bayside wetlands; it is solitary as it journeys to its winter home. As the temperature drops, the aphids thin. The ladybug vaults skyward and, aided by air currents, makes its haphazard way to a specific higher-altitude site, already crawling with others whose recent ancestors also overwintered there. Ladybugs live only several months, not long enough to have intimately known this place, so how they know where to go is a mystery.

We humans do not diapause or hibernate ourselves; the closest we come to it is sleeping, an intensely private and ritualized affair for us. Though we know better, we find ourselves projecting again: something about those pretty beetles—the noticeably slowing effect that the cold has on them; the absence of fur and burrows, those mammalian defenses—strikes us as vulnerable. We tread lightly to protect the nakedly slumbering loveliness of ladybugs upon which we've stumbled. We leave them be and wish them well on their return journeys to the coast come spring.

Gayle Wattawa

Redwood Regional Park boasts large numbers of overwintering ladybugs each year.

Overwintering ladybugs (also opposite)

Top: Marsh wren on tule stilts
Bottom, left to right: Calling out, blue-eyed grass found in marshes

MARSH WRENS

In the bulrush and tule thickets of Coyote Hills, the diminutive marsh wren (*Cistothorus palustris*) announces its existence to anyone who will listen. A consummate songster with as many as two hundred tunes in its repertoire, the marsh wren sings songs that have been likened to the sound of a busy sewing machine, needling in and out of the tules.

Unbeknown to most, this seemingly humble bird is also an architectural powerhouse. One male marsh wren may build over twenty nests in a breeding season, both to impress the ladies and to confuse predators as to the actual whereabouts of eggs. The female marsh wren, smitten by this display of industry and skill, will carefully examine the round sedge- and bulrush-woven nests, select her favorite, and make it her own by lining the inner doorstep with the soft down of cattails or feathers. Not content with a single conquest, however, the male marsh wren will invite other females to look over his offerings, ending up with several mates, each housed in her own nest.

Two hundred songs, twenty nests, several mates, and, we may presume, many offspring—how extravagant the life of this little bird!

Sylvia Linsteadt

Marsh wren songs abound in the wetlands of Coyote Hills Regional Park throughout May and June, when males sing almost incessantly.

Marsh wren on a tule reed

Left to right: Fledgling, Coyote Hills Regional Park

Monarchs on a butterfly bush

MIGRATIONS

The whimbrel lands with a soft plunk in the water just off the Albany Bulb, drifts to the shore, and begins pressing her deeply hooked bill into the sand for little crabs. It is nearly impossible to fathom the journey she's just been on and the long way she has yet to go. She holds Arctic tundra under her wings. She may travel a total of 8,500 miles before returning home again in summer, with her mate, to her breeding and nesting grounds in the Bering Sea region. She has a map that guides her—made of instinct, of magnetic homing minerals in her very blood and bones, of mysterious bird-wisdom about which we know nothing.

There is urgency to her flight and to the migrations of all creatures. Take Arctic terns, for example: they boast the longest recorded migrations in the world, traveling from far northern Canada down the Pacific coast all the way to Antarctica, an awe-inspiring 49,000-mile round-trip. Along the way, they won't interrupt their journey for the sardines left out on the decks of fishing boats, to which the gulls flock; they know there will be food, and plenty of it, later. They have miles to go before they sleep.

Chinook salmon may travel 2,500 miles from their natal streams before returning at last to mate and die, having spent up to four years roaming the Pacific. Birth-creeks stamp a seam of knowing inside every salmon, and no matter where they've swum—be it only a few hundred miles away for a single winter, like some coho, or to far Alaskan waters for Chinook—if they aren't eaten first, they will die where their parents died, food for eagles and black bears and streamside soil.

The monarch butterfly had never been to the grove of eucalyptus trees where she just overwintered, yet she knew how to get there. Scientists believe that these butterflies have photopigments in their eye stocks that allow them to tell which way the light in the sky is polarized, from which they deduce a north–south bearing. No single monarch lives long enough to make the full circuit from the Rockies west to coastal California and back again—it takes three or four generations to complete the journey—and yet somehow knowledge of winter roosts of pine or eucalyptus, of patches of milkweed on which to lay eggs, of summer homes high up in the Rockies, is retained. Overwintering monarchs cluster close together in trees, wings closed, like gray-orange leaves. Come February, mating occurs, caterpillars become pupae, and, eventually, freshly unfurled monarchs traipse through our gardens, drinking nectar, beginning to think again of the east and their ancestral summer homes.

Not much larger than monarchs, many passerines, or songbirds, use the great Pacific Flyway from the Arctic to Baja and beyond for their yearly migrations, as do the larger whimbrels and terns. Their arrival is often heralded by a new song in the garden or the hills, rather than the dramatic landing of many wings on the Bay. The little golden-crowned sparrow, for example, arrives here from Alaska around midautumn, singing a sad, spiraling tune from the treetops. It feeds until April, when it undertakes its return journey in only twenty-nine days.

Marine mammals follow their own Pacific "flyway," which is virtually the same route as the birds', just underwater. Gray whales and humpbacks make yearly journeys from the Gulf of Alaska to Baja, heaving backs and tails out of the waves as they pass along our coast. Elephant seals do the same, only they gather on beaches in great wallowing masses, resting in the sun and sand, giving birth, and then mating. Like whale cows, elephant seal females carry babies in their wombs all the way back up to northern feeding grounds, then south again, giving birth the following year.

All of these creatures hold within them maps for long journeys that at some point bring them to our doorstep, as though it were the most mundane occurrence in the world.

Sylvia Linsteadt

Colonies of overwintering monarchs can be seen at Ardenwood Historic Farm.

Winter waterfowl over Arrowhead Marsh

Mountain lion

MOUNTAIN LIONS

To the mountain lions of the East Bay, these golden hills, oak wood-lands, and willow-lined creeks comprise not a series of Regional Parks but a patchwork of tightly fitted territories. To *Puma concolor couguar,* this land is defined not by trails or county boundaries but by scat and scrape, in urine-soaked scent posts recognized only by others of their kind and perhaps other small mammals in the vicinity. They roam enormous territories, from forty to two hundred square miles. Adult males require the most space, females less, depending on the abundance of prey—which is not much of an issue here, given that Californian cougars specialize in hunting mule deer, in particular the old and the infirm.

Male mountain lions rarely tolerate territorial overlap with other males. Where land is limited, they share territory corners every so often, but not happily, and they have been known to kill infringing younger males, even their own offspring; hence the pressure that drives subadult males into suburban trees or backyards, or finds them dead along the sides of freeways. Female mountain lions will overlap territory with each other and a few males for mating purposes, but in general these cats are utterly solitary.

They are also incredibly adaptable, inhabiting virtually every ecosystem in the Americas, from the swamps of Florida to the deserts of California, from the Sierra peaks to the redwood forests. This perhaps explains the mountain lion's survival through two centuries of bounty hunting. (On the West Coast, the early-twentieth-century preservation of large swathes of wilderness has no doubt helped.) And unlike other large predators, such as wolves and grizzlies, mountain lions tend to stay high and dry of human settlements. They may every now and then take a cow or a sheep out of desperation, but most of them keep far away from us, at most a black-tipped tail vanishing around the next bend. As for the mass extinctions of megafauna that occurred during the Pleistocene some ten thousand years ago, it's believed that the mountain lion didn't escape the fate of all the other big cats in North America: recent studies suggest that a population of South American cougars repopulated this country.

As we walk the dusty trails through bay forest or open hill, we've all been touched by those stunningly beautiful feline eyes—green, amber, gold—while passing, without realizing it, through the newly established territory of a young male, or of a mother with her two speckled, smudge-faced cubs. Mountain lions stalk silently, chasing down their prey with short bursts of speed. They have small lungs and hearts, meaning that they can't bound after a deer for long, like a pack of wolves might. Rather, they must sneak up, fluid gold and silent as a soft wind, unseen and unheard until the last possible moment, and then kill with a single powerful bite to the back of the neck.

After slitting open the abdomen of their prey and removing the stomach with surgical precision, mountain lions feast on the heart and the lungs, the most nutrient-dense organs. Their whole digestive system, extremely short for a creature of their size, is designed solely for the purpose of processing meat. They ingest grass only to purge or to loosen a hairball. In his book *The Others: How Animals Made Us Human,* ecologist Paul Shepard beautifully describes the mountain lion's sister-cat the leopard as "a kind of deliverer for its prey," a beast at the very pinnacle of the food chain, the great transference of the sun's energy from plant to bird, plant to insect, plant to deer, and eventually to the "pure meat eaters[…]lying in wait on tree limbs." Mountain lions, too, are always languidly watching, reminding us of the meaning of grace, and of humility.

Sylvia Linsteadt

Continuous tracts of wilderness large enough to support stable mountain lion populations are found around Redwood, Tilden, and Diablo Foothills Regional Parks.

Left and right: Adult mountain lions

Turkey tails

MUSHROOMS

Every year, when the rains hail in winter, our East Bay fungi bloom in a dizzying array of decompositional beauty.

There are jellies that look like wet alien fingers sticking up from the ground. And coral mushrooms, true to their name, give damp forest floors the illusion of underwater reefs. Chicken of the woods appear like orange and yellow plumage sprouting from the trunks of trees, as though a Technicolor chicken climbed halfway in and got stuck. Fly amanitas are straight out of fairytale books, their spotted red caps and thick white stalks as poisonous as witches' apples. Matsutakes are dense and hard, like white stones, and their flesh smells unmistakably of dirty socks and cinnamon chewing gum.

Some of these are parasitic fungi, simply taking nutrients from trees. Other mushrooms have soul-mate relationships to specific trees, and their fidelity is part of a symbiotic connection. Queen boletes, black trumpets (which look like velvet lilies in moss), candy caps, and golden chanterelles will live with only certain live oaks, tan oaks, or pines. They are mycorrhizal fungi, lacing their thin roots through the duff below the trees, breaking down the fallen leaves or needles to sustain themselves on the sugars of photosynthesis. What we recognize as a mushroom is the fruit body of an underground cloud of mycelium, thin strands that branch out from fungi roots like vast spider silk. In return for the sugars, the mycelium deliver to the trees nitrogen and phosphates and filter heavy metals from the soil that would poison their tree companions. This allows trees to grow faster and to better weather frost and disease. The greater the diversity of trees in a forest, the greater the diversity of its mushrooms.

Jack-o'-lanterns

Left to right: Shaggy parasol, deadly amanita

Forests are not mushrooms' only home. Blewits, morels, and shaggy parasols love the space at the edge of urban decay. They are the punk kids of the fungi world, hanging around construction sites, parking lots, and suburban backyards. Their fruit even has a punk rock look—blue topped, black and wrinkled, and fringed with spiky white caps, respectively. The dead man's foot is black and hard and looks a little like dry dog droppings. It is strong enough to push through asphalt and dyes fabric lovely shades of violet.

For sheer nighttime drama, the bioluminescent jack-o'-lantern mushroom steals the show. Feathering out from the wood, its orange- and green-tinged gills shine at night like a Halloween pumpkin. It glows most brightly at the height of its spore production, brilliant and poisonous. Lamentably, it looks enough like the delectable chanterelle that unwitting mushroom eaters are tricked into hallucinations and digestive horrors. The basket stinkhorn, too, has a predilection for our Mediterranean climate and glows like the jack-o'-lantern, but its open-weave geometric body oozes a rotten meat smell that attracts flies and deters hungry hikers.

There is a slew of little brown mushrooms with fascinating lives. *Camarophyllopsis foetens* is brown, hard to tell apart from other mushrooms, and rare enough not to have a common name. Its distinct mothball smell comes from the insecticide that it produces. Springtime amanitas have veils that grow at the bottom of their stalks, so they appear to be growing out of a splash of milk. Death caps, another amanita, are similarly capped, veiled, brownish-white, ordinary looking, and the number-one cause of mushroom poisoning fatalities in the world. Candy caps set themselves apart by smelling like maple syrup and tasting like brown sugar.

At a recent mycological fair in Berkeley, 215 species of East Bay wild mushrooms were collected. For walkers who gaze downward, the world of fungal blooms tests the range of credibility.

Lindsie Bear

The best time to find mushrooms is on a sunny day following a rainy period. This is purely a spectator sport in the East Bay Regional Parks, where it is illegal to pick them.

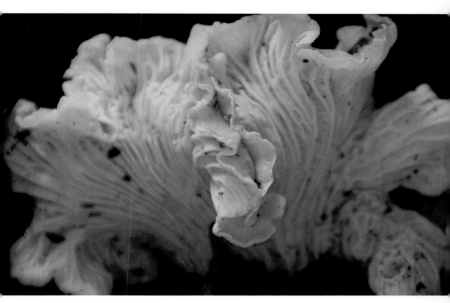

Chanterelles

Newt

NEWTS

Through the dry summer months until the first rains, the hills are full of dreaming newts, deep in aestivation. Like bears responding to winter cold, newts and salamanders lower their metabolism and hunker down in damp, rotten logs, moist gopher burrows, or deep piles of leaf litter when the ponds and creeks dry up. Summer is their winter, a time when resources are few and they are in danger of drying out.

These aestivating habits may be the source of ancient associations between salamanders (of which newts are a subgroup) and fire, an idea first put forth in writing by Pliny the Elder when he claimed that salamanders could extinguish fire with their cool skin. Imagine a rotten log thrown on a fire, a common enough sight. Rudely startled from their dreams, aestivating salamanders flee the flames, and it might appear as though they actually resided in the fire itself. Leonardo Da Vinci himself claimed that salamanders could only regenerate their skins by the heat of a flame.

While our most common salamander, the California newt (*Taricha tarosa*), boasts a fire-orange belly, these creatures are about as far from fire as can be. They are amphibians, after all, born in egg masses attached to underwater plant stalks, spending their first months with gills, and bound to the wet places of the world. If anything, it would appear that our own California newt—as well as our six other native salamander species—lives in rain, not fire. It is the first winter rains, soaking through the grass and dry dirt, that rouse slumbering newts, salamanders, and frogs from their summertime stillness and spur great mating migrations. The newts and salamanders leave tiny trails, delicate brushstrokes of ancient calligraphy, as they slowly make their way toward the breeding creeks

Newt close-up

Left to right: Rough-skinned newt with eggs, rough-skinned newt eggs

and ponds of their ancestors. Some travel only a few yards; others may journey over a mile and a half, which might take more than a month for a little newt.

You'd think, moving at such a gentle pace, that the newts wouldn't stand a chance of making it to the swollen creeks before a happy heron or fox scarfed them down. However, California newts contain a substance in their skin called tetrodotoxin (the fire-orange belly is a warning flag for predators) that affects and in some cases paralyzes vertebrates, except the garter snake. The California newt's most sinister predator is in fact the car. Cars that have access to newt-crossed roads wreak slaughter upon these slow-moving creatures. In Tilden Park, South Park Drive is closed from November 1 to April 1, restoring to newts their ancient rights-of-way as they move toward the creeks and ponds.

The long walk and the dangerous roads are worth it, though: the newts enter an ecstatic mating frenzy once they hit the water, transforming from awkward land crawlers to magnificent, keel-tailed dancers. Males patrol the creek edges sporting their mating "attire"—bright colors and little nuptial pads on their toes to grip females during amplexus. When the females arrive, the males release pheromones from their tails that drive the females to distraction. Chin rubbing and a gentle massage with the back feet further seduce female newts. Males sometimes form orgiastic mating balls around a single female, all trying to coax her to take their spermatophores at once, which she then uses to fertilize her subsequently laid egg mass. Alas, this overzealous practice sometimes leads to the drowning of the female.

Fertilized egg sacs are carefully attached to rocky crevices or plant roots and left there to grow and flourish on their own. After hatching, newts spend their larval stage in their natal pond or stream eddy until it begins to dry and they metamorphose into their terrestrial phase. Then the summer hills fill once again with secret aestivation dreams.

Sylvia Linsteadt

California newts can be found, emerging with the first rains, among the logs and leaf litter of Briones Regional Park.

Newt

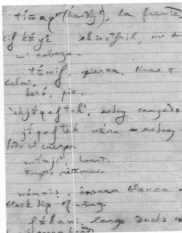

Top: José Guzman, center
Bottom, left to right: Maria de los Angeles Colos, sample of José
Guzman's Chochenyo records

OHLONE
LANGUAGE

When the pioneering anthropologist Alfred Kroeber published his then-definitive work *Handbook of the Indians of California* in 1925, he characterized the Ohlone cultures of the Bay Area as "extinct so far as all practical purposes are concerned," and indeed most citizens of this region would probably have agreed. Drawn into the missions in the last decades of the eighteenth and first decades of the nineteenth century, decimated by disease, slavery, and violence, their territory overrun by colonists of European descent, the native people of the East Bay seemed to have disappeared. As far as most residents of the Bay Area were concerned, these people were past tense, and all that remained of them were shellmounds—heaps of discarded shells, manufactured household objects, and burials scattered throughout the area, the results of thousands of years of habitation. One such shellmound, measuring four hundred by three hundred feet in area and ten feet in height, was at Coyote Hills in Fremont, and shortly after the East Bay Regional Park District acquired the land in 1967, its enterprising naturalists rebuilt some native houses to give an idea of what the villages might have looked like and to serve as props for their interpretive programs.

While much cultural knowledge had disappeared, however, the Ohlone are far from extinct, and beginning in 1994 Coyote Hills began to host an annual Gathering of Ohlone Peoples to pay tribute to what remains and to help revive what has been lost. These gatherings, along with other individual and community efforts, have resulted in what can only be described as a miracle—the return of native arts, customs, beliefs, and even language to the East Bay. Many individuals and many families have been engaged. Vincent Medina, a young Ohlone man brought up in San Leandro, expresses some of the emotion, drama, and beauty involved in bringing back the Chochenyo Ohlone language.

Malcolm Margolin

Our language almost vanished from the Earth. In 1929, in the midst of this tragedy, an aging man living in the deep brown canyons of Sunol named José Guzman proclaimed with defiance, *"Kaana 'akwe ta-k juwa ta-k nonwente,"* "As for me, I am not going to stop speaking."

José, along with the elderly Maria de los Angeles Colos, known to family and friends as Angela, worked frantically to record, speak, and protect Chochenyo, the language spoken in the East Bay since time immemorial, which was on the brink of death, the precipice of never being used again. What a world that must have been. I can only imagine, but my heart begins to ache at the thought.

These people—my elders, my heroes—made a conscious decision to keep speaking Chochenyo and to fight against time, as though in defiance of gravity. They knew they were the only ones who could protect the language, and they lunged, ducked, and leapt over the hurdles of reality in order to keep the flicker of light from moving into ashes and darkness. Angela and José weren't going out without a fight.

Yellow parchment papers became full of frantic scribbles, an outpouring of heartbreak, family histories, gossip, lore, and stories that stretched back to the beginning of time, described with such immediacy that they seemed to have happened yesterday; tales of

Opposite: Recreated Ohlone *tuppentak* (roundhouse) at Coyote Hills Regional Park

a time when giants roamed the Earth, Coyote left his footprints, bodies of stone were defeated in the underworld, and songs were sung about Mount Diablo. *Don't forget this,* I picture them saying. *Don't give up on this.*

Oh, glorious fighters, stubborn ancestors, people of defiance, people of wisdom, gravity breakers. Today, as a result of your refusal to surrender language, we as modern Ohlone can speak words once again. Because of the scribbles on parchment paper, the land hears Chochenyo a second time. It has been inside us all along. The words caress us like a grandmother, comfort us like a song, and bring us dignity and connect us to the East Bay, the place we love. My elders, my heroes, you saved it from ever being forgotten. We will not relinquish Chochenyo, for it thrives in the footsteps of giants.

Vincent Medina

Many Ohlone archeological sites are preserved within East Bay Regional Parks. Two-thousand-year-old shellmounds can be found in Coyote Hills Regional Park, while in other places village sites, mortar holes, and ten-thousand-year-old rock art stand as witness to millennia of human habitation. The Gathering of Ohlone Peoples is held at Coyote Hills every October.

Rock walls in Mission Peak Regional Preserve

ROCK WALLS

Spread randomly throughout the East Bay hills are disconnected stretches of rock walls, beginning nowhere in particular, ending nowhere in particular, and serving no conceivable purpose. How deliciously exasperating! If nothing else, we humans are a story-making species, made deeply uneasy by any phenomenon that doesn't fit into a story, a history, a scientific theory. Although these walls are rarely more than a couple of feet high, they have stubbornly withstood the challenges of the human mind to conquer them. Who built them and why? There must be an answer, and for more than a century various people, known collectively as "wall-nuts," have been setting their minds to the task of explanation.

Among the more wild ideas is that the walls were astronomical markers put here by ancient Chinese explorers. There have been dark rumors of an ancient, pre-Indian civilization with great cities and advanced technologies. I have even heard it suggested that the walls were guides for the spaceships of extraterrestrial visitors. I really don't know about any of this. I won't make a big point of it—I hate to be one to squelch the imagination—but I personally tend to dismiss these lines of speculation as the flamboyance and silliness of a world whose tastes are so jaded that only the utterly theatrical and garish can rouse the mind to interest.

What are my own ideas about these walls? In truth, I still don't have any. It was hardly typical of the Indian people of this area to move rocks and build walls. It has been suggested that they might have been sheep pens, but they do not form enclosures the way sheep pens should. Since these high and dry hills were surely never farmed, I doubt if the rocks were moved to make the ground ready for plowing, as was the case in New England fields. They do not

Top, bottom, and opposite: Mission Peak Regional Preserve

follow tribal boundaries, nor the property lines of either the Spanish land grants or the Anglo ranches that followed them.

I do not know why these rocks were hauled up to the ridgetops and aligned this way. I do not know who put them here, or when. And, to be honest, I find that I enjoy not knowing. This past is indeed a strange country, and I love to explore it less for the knowledge it reveals than for the mysteries it holds.

Malcolm Margolin

Sections of these mysterious walls still remain in Tilden and Sibley Regional Parks and Mission Peak Regional Preserve, waiting to be found by intrepid explorers.

Coyote Hills Regional Park salt ponds

SAN FRANCISCO BAY

In the early 1960s, San Francisco Bay was on its way to being filled within an inch of its watery existence. With 90 percent of the historic tidal marshes gone, it seemed there was no stopping progress. Plans called for lopping off mountains, dumping the dirt in the Bay, building more houses and more freeways, and growing the population of the region to a seam-busting fourteen million by 2020. It seemed no amount of asphalt was too much.

Then a trio of determined homemakers from Berkeley stepped in. Fed up with the sight of dump trucks pouring dirt on tidal marshes and construction cranes poised at the water's edge, they took action. When the region's high-powered conservation leaders deferred help because they were too busy saving the redwoods and the remote mountains, Kay Kerr, Sylvia McLaughlin, and Esther Gulick concluded, "We'll do it ourselves." On stylish letterhead, the fledgling Save San Francisco Bay Association rallied neighbors, parishioners, Berkeley faculty, and their well-connected spouses. Mr. Kerr, as it happened, ran the University of California.

Grassroots in the truest sense, Save the Bay persevered until local and then national legislation made it impossible to develop wetlands and shorelines without extensive scrutiny. Why did they do it? Someone had to. Someone had to step forward, and three

Top: View from Hayward Regional Shoreline
Bottom, left to right: San Francisco Bay with Golden Gate Bridge, jackrabbit

savvy, tenacious, extraordinary women took it upon themselves. For the children. For the future. For the simple love of a beautiful sunset or a living landscape.

Marilee Enge

Today, McLaughlin Eastshore State Park, named for Save the Bay's cofounder Sylvia McLaughlin, protects eight and a half miles of the Bay's shoreline and is the unique product of regional, municipal, and private collaboration.

San Francisco Bay at sunset

Phacelia

SEEDS

It's spring, and the poppies, lupines, phacelias, clarkias, larkspurs, paintbrushes, blue dicks, columbines, shooting stars, Chinese houses, and a host of other wildflowers explode over the East Bay meadowlands, dazzling the eye and gladdening the heart. It's one of life's great shows, seemingly spontaneous but in reality the result of eons of careful experimentation and development. Since flowering plants first emerged over a hundred million years ago, these showy wildflowers have been intensely engaged in an ongoing study of the minds of bees, butterflies, hummingbirds, and other pollinators, evolving blooms with a stunning variety of colors and shapes that will attract their attention, seduce them, and for a fleeting moment enslave them to the plant's need.

Other flowering plants, however—especially trees and grasses—have adopted a different strategy, releasing pollen into the air and counting on the winds to make the necessary connections. Without the need to attract pollinators, their flowers are plain, often rudimentary, but because of the hit-or-miss quality of wind pollination, generally more plentiful.

As the flowers of spring fall away, and the heat, dryness, and long days of summer follow, yet another wonderment emerges: seeds. Each species of flowering plant has had to evolve a strategy to assure the survival and dispersal of its seeds. They have had to create coatings to protect the embers of life from drought and rot; they have had to develop safeguards to prevent germination at the wrong time; and they have had to devise a way of dispersing the seeds to new locations. In addition to wind, water and animals help seeds in their locomotion, and some seeds even seem blessed with their own means of movement.

Arroyo willow

Coast sedge

Oak mistletoe

Our native bigleaf maple, *Acer macrophyllum,* has copper-colored, helicopter-shaped seedpods that spring winds wrest free from branches. Their spiraling path rarely takes them far from the mother tree, keeping them close to water-rich soils.

The wind can carry the fluffy, white-haired seeds of the arroyo willow (*Salix lasiolepis*) many miles away, though these riparian plants hedge their bets with seeds that are also buoyant and can travel far downstream on the surface of the water. Willows wisely wait until after the winter and spring rains to release their seeds, which might otherwise find themselves buried too deeply when floods disturb the soil.

The marsh-loving coast sedge (*Carex obnupta*), beloved of California Indian basket weavers for the fine fibers of its rhizomes, encases each of its angular seeds in a pocket of air so that it can float on the water like a canoe.

Oak mistletoe (*Phoradendron villosum*), the chartreuse-green "kissing plant" of the solstice season, has sticky white berries that are toxic to all but the birds that adore them. Inside the berries are seeds with tough outer membranes; they wouldn't break down if digested, a common way for seeds to travel. However, what happens more frequently with oak mistletoe is that the seeds, sticky with berry pulp, cling to birds' feet and are thus carried to their new homes between the toes of these avian songsters.

In a bad year, a coast live oak (*Quercus agrifolia*) may lose all of its nuts to hungry squirrels, jays, deer, and even people. It relies on caching animals like scrub jays and squirrels to spread its glossy seeds: scrub jays, for example, will gather and bury up to five thousand acorns in a six-acre radius each fall. Though the jays only forget the locations of around 5 percent of these, the acorns have already been thoughtfully buried under a half-inch of soil and thus germination rates are favorable.

Bigleaf maple

Coast live oak

California oatgrass

California oatgrass (*Danthonia californica*), a perennial bunchgrass common in coastal prairie habitats, is a favorite of all grazing animals for its sweet, nutritious seeds. The seeds have developed a way to "walk" by way of appendages called awns. Similar to fine bristles, awns twist and untwist as moisture is absorbed or depleted, allowing the seed to slowly wriggle, in a corkscrew fashion, deeper and deeper into the soil until thoroughly planted.

Each seed is a tiny masterwork of engineering and architecture as varied, as surprising, and in many ways as beautiful as the flower from which it sprang.

Malcolm Margolin and Sylvia Linsteadt

Throughout spring and summer, the East Bay trails and parks are alive with germination. Sunol Regional Wilderness is a particularly beautiful spot to see wildflowers bursting open to disperse their seeds.

Top: Wilson's warbler
Bottom, left to right: Great horned owl, tree frog

SOUNDSCAPES

Rising up from the oak and bay forest along Wildcat Creek Trail at dawn is a robust chorus of chirrups, trills, lilts, swishes, creaks, and croaks. It is a perfect example of what eminent soundscape ecologist Bernie Krause calls biophony, or, in more metaphorical language, "The Great Animal Orchestra." That dawn chorus, according to Krause, is not just a lovely and chaotic net of sound. It is also rich with information, every bit as symphonic as our own orchestral songs. Each bird, for example, has found a sonic niche over the millennia in which to sing and chat and call out warnings so that others of its kind can distinguish its voice. What's more, the web of sound is not only highly complex (when an ecosystem is healthy and full) but also pleasing to the ear. It would be foolish to deny that our own music arose from this very orchestra, conceived among the hush of creeks, the high hums of bats, the hoots of owls.

In some respects, however, these sounds are more like sung language than they are like notes played on flutes. Take Pacific tree frogs, for example, who abound in little ponds and seeps throughout the East Bay Regional Parks. The croaks of frogs, common after a storm, not only ring out on their own "sonic bandwidth" in the ongoing chorus but also confuse predators so that the hunting coyote or hawk has no idea where to locate a single frog. The ribbit-splash of one frightened frog can cause the whole lot to go silent on a dime. Those frog-songs are thus both symphonic and encoded with meaning.

The sounds you hear while walking through a forest—a junco cheeping high and gentle, a blue jay scolding—and dismiss as background noise are actually an ongoing conversation. That afternoon frenzy of birdcalls or morning exuberance of songs is also:

Top: Song sparrow
Bottom: Gray fox

spotted towhee mates checking in to make sure the other is safe; a blue jay calling out about a bobcat sneaking through the brush; a robin asserting his territory; and a junco alerting everyone that you are coming. Have you ever wondered why you never seem to be able to get close to a doe, gray fox, or coyote? It's because they knew you were coming five minutes ago: the birds told them. The birds keep tabs on everyone passing through their home, calling out about it, moment by moment, from dusk to dawn. They narrate, in real time, the story of their particular swathe of land.

Sylvia Linsteadt

The biophonic Wildcat Creek Trail can be experienced in Wildcat Canyon Regional Park and the Tilden Nature Area. A sunrise hike up Mission Peak is another sure way to experience beautiful vistas and mellifluous soundscapes.

Left to right: Mule deer, dark-eyed junco

TILDEN MERRY-GO-ROUND

A chestnut mare, nostrils wide with fear, is only ever a gallop away from the jaws of a dragon at Tilden's Herschell-Spillman Merry-Go-Round, where children's delighted squeals seem integral to the calliope soundtrack. Built in New York in 1911, this thrilling menagerie-model carousel is a rare example of bygone craftsmanship.

Though there is nothing funereal about these robust animals, they were lovingly assembled by way of "coffin construction," meaning that craftsmen glued together six or seven poplar-wood boxes, one for each section of the body, making everything lighter and easier to transport. Watch for seams where a head or a leg meets a body.

Life-sized sketches guided three classes of carvers, all of whom did their work by hand: the straightforward legs were given to young apprentices; the more elaborate bodies to journeymen; and

Tilden Regional Park's Herschell-Spillman Merry-Go-Round (*also opposite*)

Top and bottom: Details of Tilden Merry-Go-Round

those emotive, finely chiseled heads were entrusted to the master carvers, who also finessed transitions and added finishing touches of musculature. The animals were then painstakingly hand painted.

Animals on the outermost ring are the fanciest, particularly their "romance," or outward-facing, profiles, which seduce onlookers with detail—lustrous manes, brightly colored bows, golden saddle tassels—though the animals and profiles that keep shyly to the interior are very nearly as lovely. In addition to the classic horse (note the real horsehair tails), the Herschell-Spillman Company created fourteen whimsical menagerie models, all of which are present on the Tilden carousel: cat, deer, dragon, frog, giraffe, goat, pig, rooster, stork, tiger, zebra, lion, and dog. Only one of these sports clothing (accessories do not count)—can you spot it? (Hint: The outfit may have been inspired by *The Wind in the Willows.*)

Discerning riders will notice that something is different about the innermost ring of creatures: added in 1950, these beasts are cast aluminum, more typical of the industry after the heyday of handcraftsmanship had collapsed, along with the nation's stock markets. The Tilden Merry-Go-Round is on the National Register of Historic Places, and it has a younger sister, also built by Herschell-Spillman, in Golden Gate Park.

As beautiful as this antique is on its own, the true wonderment is the gleam in a child's eye upon beholding it, a force as necessary as any craftsman's skill to turn wood and paint into something magical.

Gayle Wattawa

Hours for Tilden Regional Park's Merry-Go-Round are posted on the East Bay Regional Park District's website.

TURKEY VULTURES

"It's only a vulture."

How many times have we said or thought this when a hoped-for golden eagle, osprey, or red-tailed hawk turns out to be a run-of-the-mill turkey vulture? Their appetite for carrion and their naked, rumpled faces admittedly give these scavenging birds an unsettling demeanor, but they are remarkable animals.

Vultures are the only animals in the world known to have stomach enzymes and immune systems strong enough to destroy bacteria and viruses, from anthrax and botulinum to E. coli, so when they ingest a rotting corpse, they are filtering bacteria out of their ecosystem before it can hit the water and soil. This trait is reflected in their Latin name, *Cathartes aura,* which means golden purifier or purifying breeze.

The name is apt on other levels. Vultures are known to hunt by riding hot updrafts of breeze, smelling their way to sites of death

Turkey vulture (also opposite)

Top and bottom: Turkey vulture wingspan

and decay; they are the only North American bird with a developed olfactory sense. At the same time, and unlike most birds, vultures don't have vocal organs. Instead of soul-piercing shrieks, celebratory chirps, and bellowing caws, the vulture can only issue hisses when alarmed and deep, soulful grunts and groans when nesting and wooing a partner. All of this silent energy is centered instead on finding their meals. Surprising as it may be, given their taste in food, vultures are very clean animals. They bathe often in water, thereby easily cleansing their bald, pink faces. They preen obsessively and hold their wings open in the sun to bake off the bacteria.

It's harder than you'd think to find a good meal, and hikers will see groups of circling vultures above bare, golden ridges. (The collective noun for flying vultures is a kettle, and indeed the scene is reminiscent of liquid swirling in an old metal pot.) Coasting on those hot thermals, they keep at least one other vulture in sight and fly in that configuration until one of them spots carrion. Then, one by one, like dominoes, the vultures dip down to the site of the carcass. Since it can take a while to find a feast, riding thermals saves energy, though it means that by dusk, the hunt is over. Come nightfall, turkey vultures return to shared roosts, many of which have been used for more than a century.

So, instead of feeling disappointed when we recognize their silvery, V-winged silhouettes, let us rejoice that our "golden purifiers" are alive and well. The Cherokee Nation calls vultures "Peace Eagles": though they look like other raptors from afar, they do not kill. They only scavenge, and thus cleanse.

Sylvia Linsteadt

Turkey vultures can be found soaring throughout California, but they are most easily viewed from high, open places, such as the ridgetop parks of Bishop Ranch Regional Preserve.

Vasco Caves Regional Preserve vernal pool

VERNAL POOLS

Through the drought of California's summer months, everything in the vernal pool lies dormant, waiting—the larvae of the fairy shrimp, the seeds of Contra Costa goldfield and sand-spurrey wildflowers. Then, for a brief moment in spring, the pool comes to life. It transforms from a flat patch of scrubby grass or swathe of cracked earth into a stunning disc of colorful blooms and a nursery of amphibians and crustaceans. (Since predatory fish require year-round water, vernal pools are unusually safe places for eggs of amphibians and crustaceans.)

Bees of the family *Adrenidae* nest in the nearby ground in tiny burrows and emerge en masse to pollinate the fleeting blooms of the meadowfoam and downingia, ensuring their emergence the following year. Winter and spring waters bring to life crustaceans whose eggs sacs have been suspended, like chaparral seeds waiting for fire, since the previous year. It is thought that these "cyst-stage"

Vernal pools at Coyote Hills Regional Park

Top: Vernal pools at Coyote Hills Regional Park
Bottom, left to right: Downingia flowers, Vasco Caves Regional Preserve

eggs could survive for centuries in the dry earth: perhaps there are fairy shrimp eggs still waiting for a wet season in some vernal pool long dry.

Vernal pools wax and wane yearly as the moon does, each flower and toad and feather-shaped fairy shrimp marking the quick passage of time. What's more, the hardpan bottoms of these pools may be imprints of Ice Age abundance, formed by the stomping feet and wallowing bodies of California's own Pleistocene Columbian mammoths. Extant megafauna, such as African elephants and bison, create similar depressions, rolling and rubbing their bodies until caked in mud, then shimmying against rocks and trees to scrape off the dried residue (and with it any ectoparasites). Though the mammoths are now extinct, the wallows they stomped and rubbed into the earth continue to host a magnificent and ephemeral tangle of life.

Sylvia Linsteadt

Endangered fairy shrimp can be found on the rocky outcrops of Vasco Caves Regional Preserve, where vernal pools accumulate in the winter and spring months.

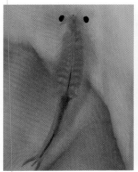 

Left to right: Fairy shrimp, fringed downingia

Sibley Volcanic Regional Preserve

VOLCANOES

It is easy to forget that we are walking on a thin skin of soil, dirt, and rock that is floating, like the buttery crust of potpie, on a sea of liquid magma. On a human scale, it all seems sturdy enough, save for the infrequent earthquake. But in the span of geologic time, the surface of the earth is buoyed by molten rock, which every so often erupts into volcanoes and reminds us that we walk on fire. We don't think of the East Bay as volcano country, but at Sibley Volcanic Regional Preserve, the late 1940s quarrying efforts of Kaiser Sand and Gravel Company have exposed the slit-open heart of a volcano.

The prostrate volcano at Sibley, called Round Top, is one of a group of four volcanoes that formed some ten million years ago, when three-toed horses and American camels were hitting their stride as grassland grazers. Back then, the land that would one day comprise the rippled East Bay hills was hitched to a juncture of tectonic plates near San Jose that forced it ever north. Round Top and its siblings were born from the immense pressure of three colliding and subducting plates—the Pacific, North American, and Gorda. When dense oceanic plate turned to magma, it shot through the crust, up veins and out vents like Round Top.

It is not often that one has the chance to peer under the earth's skin and behold magma arteries, and it is rarer still to lay eyes on a volcano, in all of its once-fiery strength, laid flat like a felled tree by shifting fault lines. When you reach the edge of the old quarry, look down. Your gaze will be met with the heart of a volcano, though turned on its side: outcrops of basaltic lava layered with ash, once horizontal, are now vertical. This is hard proof that a volcano can be born, and then die, and that its bones, sidelong, can be dragged

Sibley Volcanic Regional Preserve

north inside the moving earth. For a split second, while a mother pushes a baby stroller past and a raven dives down to the labyrinth at the base of the quarry, eternity flashes. We see these sideways stripes of red basalt and this dusty mass of rock and dirt and behold a mythically imagined volcano, ten million years dead.

Sylvia Linsteadt

Sibley Volcanic Regional Preserve, an excellent spot to view volcanic rocks of the Moraga Formation, is also home to several man-made labyrinths in a unique wilderness setting.

Labyrinth at Sibley Volcanic Regional Preserve

Western pond turtles

WESTERN
POND TURTLES

"Slow and steady wins the race," Aesop tells us, as the patient, plodding tortoise of myth trudges onward, lumbering step by lumbering step, eventually snatching victory from the speedy but fidgety hare. No wonder. Hares, like all of us mammals, are evolution's most recent, newfangled idea; all the kinks haven't been worked out yet. Tortoises and turtles, however, are of a mysterious and unresolved lineage that goes back more than 220 million years to a time before lizards, snakes, or crocodiles—indeed, to a time when the life forms known as dinosaurs were still freshly created. Covering themselves with a hard, rigid shell, they exchanged nimbleness for safety, then hunkered down for the long haul. It was a most successful exchange. As other animals of equal antiquity have vanished, the turtle has persevered, a clear winner in the evolutionary race for survival. Individual turtles are among the most long-lived of all animals, with members of some species reaching 150 years.

Our own native turtle, the western pond turtle (*Actinemys marmorata*), found in certain ponds and waterways in places like Morgan Territory and Black Diamond Mines, seems, like other members of its clan, to be likewise unhurried. It matures slowly, not ready for reproduction until it is about eleven years old, and it can live more than thirty years. Why rush things?

But all is not peaceful, even here. One of the most unusual sights our area offers is the opportunity to witness a grand battle

Western pond turtle (also opposite)

among the turtles, complete with biting, shoving, and ferocious open-mouth displays. What are they fighting about? Food? Mates? No, no, no. Let us remember that these are turtles. They are fighting over desirable basking spots—the limited space on a log or a rock; they are fighting over the best place in which to take a nap in the sun.

Malcolm Margolin

An exceedingly rare creature, the western pond turtle can be found throughout the wildlife corridor between Mount Diablo and Black Diamond Mines Regional Preserve.

Grasses waving in the wind at Coyote Hills Regional Park

WIND

What could be simpler? Two air fronts meet each other: a cold, condensed, high-pressure area out over the ocean and a warmer, lighter, low-pressure area hovering above the inland valleys. To resolve the resulting tension—nature abhors a vacuum—air moves from high to low, and the result is our prevailing west-to-east winds here in the East Bay. This seemingly mechanical action has a profound impact on the landscape.

Wind shapes the seeds of plants so they can be carried aloft. It coaxes branches of trees, stems of flowers, and blades of grass to be supple enough to withstand it without breaking. It scours caves in the ridgetops of Las Trampas Regional Wilderness. It makes oak trees grow sidelong, their branches like billowing hair, on the windiest hills. Crows and ravens somersault and play on its gusts, and turkey vultures ride its warm updrafts in search of carrion. Wind, combined with the pull of the moon, shapes the ocean, making waves crash and foam; turning the Bay gray-brown with movement on a dark and windy day; creating the deeper gyres and currents of our nutrient-rich offshore upwelling.

Our prevailing, ocean-born winds are not the winds of hurricanes or tornadoes but are gentle and insistent in their shaping of the land. Without wind, the air would be stale and still and full of smog. Clouds would not drift gently by in great white caravans. Kites could not be borne aloft at Miller/Knox Regional Shoreline. After all, in both Latin and Sanskrit, the words for soul and wind are one and the same—*anima* and *atman,* respectively. Those gusts on our cheeks, that soft but constant motion of air through the

trees, are perhaps nothing less than the soul of the sky, passing through.

Sylvia Linsteadt

Carved by wind, the stone outcroppings on Rocky Ridge in Las Trampas Regional Wilderness are now home to a beautiful array of colorful lichen.

Top: Grasses waving in the wind at Coyote Hills Regional Park
Opposite: Coyote Hills Regional Park salt ponds with ripples at sunset

Woodrat

WOODRATS

There is a dense stretch of willows and dogwoods just before Jewel Lake in Tilden Nature Area where the woodrat nests are so frequent—one or two for every bend along the wooden walkway—it seems like a kingdom. Hoarded within these structures are treasuries of glinting scraps—candy wrappers, metal pen caps, pennies—testaments to the packrat's love of shininess.

Some dusky-footed woodrat (*Neotoma fuscipes*) nests are so large that a child, or even a small adult, could fit comfortably inside their bulk (if they were hollow, which they are not). Given that most nests are occupied by one woodrat at a time, save during mating and pupping seasons, these abodes are positively palatial, full of tunnels and chambers in which to stash acorns and other foods, as well as their prized collections. Their sheer size is thought to be a buffer against temperature changes and a deterrent for the raiding coyote, often discouraged midway through digging.

Nests are not rebuilt by new generations but rather are passed on, as an old country estate might be. As to the inheritance of these elaborate stick-pile homes, one wonders which progeny gets to take over once a mother is gone. Perhaps this is the reason for clusters of woodrat nests, where family groups spread out, some inheriting old nests, some building new, smaller ones, to which subsequent generations will add wings and towers and verandahs from willow, poison oak, and dogwood.

All those extra rooms don't go to waste: woodrats don't seem to mind boarders from other species, including lizards, frogs, insects, and deer mice, who are known to help themselves to food stores. Woodrats even keep their nest chambers fumigated

Top: Woodrat nest
Bottom: Woodrat

and parasite-free, lined by the fragrant and cleansing leaves of the California bay laurel.

Basically conical piles of sticks, the nests don't seem very sturdy, but the hearts of the nests may be thousands of years old. Urine accumulates, coating the bottom layers of the nest, and in drier southwestern desert regions, the urine crystallizes into a protective lacquer called amberat, preserving whatever traces of pollen the ancestral woodrats happened to collect at the time. These nests are thus layered stories of the vegetational changes of a landscape. In our East Bay Regional Parks as well as places in drier climes, a woodrat was just as likely to secret away an arrowhead a thousand years ago as it is wont to hoard a fallen pen cap today. Woodrats are thus unsuspecting history keepers, in whose tangled nests the present is recorded and the past is glimpsed.

Sylvia Linsteadt

Woodrats prefer to build their nests in oak- or bay-dominated woodlands. While woodrats themselves are rarely seen in the daytime, their nests are a familiar sight in Tilden Nature Area.

Fruiting bay laurel

A CONSTANT WONDER
Eighty Years of East Bay Regional Parks

On its eightieth anniversary, the East Bay Regional Park District is pleased to welcome the publication of *Wonderments of the East Bay,* an eloquent invitation to experience and explore the natural and cultural treasures of the East Bay Regional Parks. From the very start, District founders aimed for more than preservation of precious resources. They sought to provide for people's enjoyment, appreciation, and understanding of the landscape's myriad wonders.

"The area is yours to tramp over and enjoy…from deep wooded canyons to high wind-swept peaks." So began the pamphlet for one of the first District parks. "These…acres are dedicated to those who find pleasure and inspiration in observing plants and animals living under natural conditions."

The founding of the District is in itself an incredible story. Conceived during the hard times of the Great Depression, the Park District was the result of a successful public campaign to save surplus watershed lands from certain development.

A 1930 survey of potential parklands signaled what was at stake: "The charm of the region as a place in which to live will depend largely upon the natural conditions that are destined to disappear unless properly protected for the public in general…the absence of parks will make living conditions less and less attractive, less and less wholesome."

Local citizens agreed; they saw the benefits of parks for their community, their children, and their children's children. Even in that difficult era, they elected to tax themselves to preserve and protect public access to open space—creating the very first regional park agency in the nation.

A triumph at the outset, the District never stopped growing. It now stretches from Bay to Delta, spans Alameda and Contra Costa counties, and preserves over 117,000 acres of open space, 65 parks, and 1,200 miles of trails.

Park District leaders today uphold the original vision. They invite you outside to discover the wonderments in our special places.

ABOUT THE AUTHORS

Sylvia Linsteadt followed coyote tracks all the way back to her native Bay Area after attending Brown University, where she studied literary arts. She runs two stories-by-mail projects, *The Gray Fox Epistles* and *The Leveret Letters,* and her work has been published in *New California Writing 2013, The Dark Mountain Project, EarthLines Magazine,* and *News from Native California.* For more information about her ecology and myth-based writing, visit wildtalewort.com.

Malcolm Margolin is the founder and executive director of Heyday and the author/editor of several books, including *The Ohlone Way, The East Bay Out,* and *The Way We Lived: California Indian Stories, Songs, and Reminiscences.* He has received dozens of honors, including lifetime achievement awards from the San Francisco Bay Area Book Reviewers Association and the California Studies Association, a Community Leadership Award from the San Francisco Foundation, and a Cultural Freedom Award from the Lannan Foundation. In 2012 he received the Chairman's Commendation from the National Endowment for the Humanities, becoming the second person in the United States to receive the award.

HEYDAY
into California

About Heyday

Heyday is an independent, nonprofit publisher and unique cultural institution. We promote widespread awareness and celebration of California's many cultures, landscapes, and boundary-breaking ideas. Through our well-crafted books, public events, and innovative outreach programs we are building a vibrant community of readers, writers, and thinkers.

Thank You

It takes the collective effort of many to create a thriving literary culture. We are thankful to all the thoughtful people we have the privilege to engage with. Cheers to our writers, artists, editors, storytellers, designers, printers, bookstores, critics, cultural organizations, readers, and book lovers everywhere!

We are especially grateful for the generous funding we've received for our publications and programs during the past year from foundations and hundreds of individual donors. Major supporters include:

Anonymous (6); Alliance for California Traditional Arts; Arkay Foundation; Judith and Phillip Auth; Judy Avery; Paul Bancroft III; Richard and Rickie Ann Baum; Bay-Tree Fund; S. D. Bechtel, Jr. Foundation; Jean and Fred Berensmeier; Berkeley Civic Arts Program and Civic Arts Commission; Joan Berman; Nancy Bertelsen; Beatrice Bowles, in memory of Susan S. Lake; John Briscoe; Lewis and Sheana Butler; Cahill Contractors, Inc.; California Civil Liberties Public Education Program; Cal Humanities; California Indian Heritage Center Foundation; California State Parks Foundation; Joanne Campbell; Keith Campbell Foundation; John and Nancy Cassidy Family Foundation, through Silicon Valley Community Foundation; Graham Chisholm; The Christensen Fund; Jon Christensen; Community Futures Collective; Compton Foundation; Creative Work Fund; Lawrence Crooks; Nik Dehejia; Chris Desser and Kirk Marckwald; Frances Dinkelspiel and Gary Wayne; Doune Fund; The Durfee Foundation; Megan Fletcher and J.K. Dineen; Flow Fund Circle; Fulfillco; Furthur Foundation; The Wallace Alexander Gerbode Foundation; Nicola W. Gordon; Wanda Lee Graves and Stephen Duscha; The Walter and Elise Haas Fund; Coke and James Hallowell; Steve Hearst; Historic Resources Group; Sandra and Charles Hobson; Nettie Hoge; Donna Ewald Huggins; JiJi Foundation;

Claudia Jurmain; Kalliopeia Foundation; Marty and Pamela Krasney; Robert and Karen Kustel; Guy Lampard and Suzanne Badenhoop; Christine Leefeldt, in celebration of Ernest Callenbach and Malcolm Margolin's friendship; Thomas Lockard and Alix Marduel; Thomas J. Long Foundation; Sam and Alfreda Maloof Foundation for Arts & Crafts; Michael McCone; Giles W. and Elise G. Mead Foundation; Moore Family Foundation; Michael J. Moratto, in memory of Berta Cassel; Karen and Thomas Mulvaney; The MSB Charitable Fund; Richard Nagler; National Wildlife Federation; Humboldt Area Foundation, Native Cultures Fund; The Nature Conservancy; Nightingale Family Foundation; Northern California Water Association; Ohlone-Costanoan Esselen Nation; Panta Rhea Foundation; David Plant; Spreck and Isabella Rosekrans; Alan Rosenus; The San Francisco Foundation; Greg Sarris; Sierra College; Stephen Silberstein Foundation; William Somerville; Martha Stanley; Radha Stern, in honor of Malcolm Margolin and Diane Lee; Roselyne Chroman Swig; Tides Foundation; Sedge Thomson and Sylvia Brownrigg; Sonia Torres; Michael and Shirley Traynor; The Roger J. and Madeleine Traynor Foundation; Lisa Van Cleef and Mark Gunson; Patricia Wakida; John Wiley & Sons, Inc.; Peter Booth Wiley and Valerie Barth; Bobby Winston; Dean Witter Foundation; and Yocha Dehe Wintun Nation.

Board of Directors

Getting Involved

To learn more about our publications, events, membership club, and other ways you can participate, please visit www.heydaybooks.com.